Our Grandparents
A Global Album

With a foreword by **Archbishop Desmond Tutu**

Maya Ajmera

Sheila Kinkade

Cynthia Pon

A GLOBAL FUND FOR
Children
BOOK

Spain

Charlesbridge

Uzbekistan

Pépé • Mémé FRENCH

Nonno • Nonna ITALIAN

Babu • Bibi SWAHILI

Kūkū • Tūtū HAWAIIAN

YIDDISH Zayde • Bubbe

UZBEK Bobojon • Onajon

Dedushka • Babushka RUSSIAN

VIETNAMESE (MATERNAL) Ông ngoại • Bà ngoại

Australia

Vietnam

Grandpa • Grandma ENGLISH

ARABIC Jaddi • Jaddati

JAPANESE Ojiichan • Obaachan

Yeye • Nainai CHINESE (PATERNAL)

Venezuela

Abuelito • Abuelita SPANISH

Serbia

SERBIAN **Deda • Baba**

PORTUGUESE **Vovô • Vovó**

Dada • Dadi HINDI AND URDU (PATERNAL)

KOREAN **Haraboji • Halmoni**

GERMAN **Opa • Oma**

Haiti

Granpapa • Grann HAITIAN CREOLE

Foreword

Grandchildren are a wonderful gift. They allow us to see the world, once again, through the eyes of a child. We become more aware of life's simple treasures—the perfection of a spider's web, the wonders of a starfish. We laugh. We sing. We play with our grandchildren. Their joyful innocence awakens the child in us and gives us hope for the future.

As grandparents we also bear important responsibilities. Just as our grandchildren make us more present to the world around us, we must be present to them. We need to listen carefully and look them in the eye when they share their triumphs and struggles, their hopes and dreams.

Our experiences, collected over a lifetime, make us valuable teachers and mentors. What are the lessons our grandchildren most need to learn from us? Love. Compassion. Integrity. Perseverance. If we do our job well, our grandchildren will grow to have open minds and open hearts.

In our role as elders, we help bridge the present with the past. We tell stories from our own childhood of how we lived, and how times have changed. We share the old ways and time-honored traditions. We make sure that the wisdom of our ancestors is passed on to the next generation.

In watching my own grandchildren grow, I am reminded of how easily their attitudes and beliefs are shaped. Will they grow up secure in their own self-worth? Will they know limitation, or will they have the courage to soar? The love and support we give our grandchildren helps safeguard their future—and makes the world a better place.

Archbishop Desmond Tutu
Nobel Peace Prize Laureate

China (Tibet)

Our grandparents **love** us. They give the biggest hugs and hold our hands.

India

Mexico

USA

Tanzania

USA

Even when we speak softly, they listen.
They encourage us.

Saudi Arabia

USA

Grandparents **explore** the world with us.

Japan

Greenland

USA

USA

They tell good stories.
We love to read together!

Yemen

China

Grandparents **play** and laugh with us.

USA

Germany

USA

USA

Mongolia

Canada

Grandparents **teach** us what they know.

Pakistan

Italy

Together we learn
about the world
around us.

Kenya

USA

Grandparents **celebrate** with us.

Morocco

United Kingdom

USA

Russia

USA

They **share** stories about our families and traditions.

Grandparents take care of us, and we take care of them, too.

China

USA

USA

Cuba

Peru

With our grandparents we feel **happy**, **safe**, and **loved**.

USA

The grandparents and grandchildren in this book come from all over the world.

Greenland

Canada

USA

Mexico

Cuba

Haiti

Venezuela

Peru

Brazil

Chile

Chile

Jordan

United Kingdom
Denmark
Germany
Romania
Serbia
Spain
Italy
Morocco
Russia
Mongolia
Uzbekistan
China
Japan
Jordan
Saudi Arabia
Pakistan
Nepal
India
Yemen
Vietnam
Ghana
Kenya
Tanzania
Australia
South Africa

Ghana

Five Things to Do with Your Grandparents

USA

CELEBRATE THE PAST

Your grandparents grew up during a different time than you. Maybe they lived in a different town or country than they do now. Ask your grandparents to describe the place where they grew up. How was life different then? Did your grandparents have pets? Where did they go to school? Did they have a favorite book? What kinds of food did they like when they were children?

RECORD MEMORIES

Draw a picture of you and your grandmother or grandfather. Pose for a photograph together, or write a story about an activity you enjoyed together. If someone you know can record a video, make a short movie of you and your grandparent doing something special.

PLAY TOGETHER

Ask your grandparents about the games or hobbies they enjoyed as children. Did your grandfather like to fly a kite or make animals out of paper? Did your grandmother collect stamps or play an instrument? Ask your grandparents if they could teach you how to do one of the things they liked to do. You might learn how to sew, or make a birdhouse, or cook a favorite family meal.

Denmark

Brazil

PLAN AN ADVENTURE

Is there someplace special that your grand-mother or grandfather likes to go? Do you have a favorite place that you would like to share with them? Ask your grandparents to go to a park, a garden, or a beach where you can spend time together. Think of things you can do together while you are there, such as collecting leaves or making a sand castle.

LEARN ABOUT YOUR FAMILY

Grandparents teach us about our parents, aunts, uncles, cousins, great grandparents, and other people in our family. Spend an afternoon with your grandfather looking at photographs of your family from the past. Ask your grandmother to share with you something—a plate, a picture, a box—that has been in your family for many years. What makes it special? Why has she saved it?

To my nana and naniji and dada and dadiji—M. A.

For Mimi, who showed her love in so many ways—S. K.

To my grandparents and their grandparents . . . ,
for their perseverance, generosity, and love—C. P.

The authors wish to thank Elise Hofer Derstine and Hayley Crown for their collaboration in the development of this book.

Our Grandparents: A Global Album was developed by The Global Fund for Children (www.globalfundforchildren.org), a nonprofit organization committed to advancing the dignity of children and youth around the world. Global Fund for Children books teach young people to value diversity and help them become productive and caring citizens of the world.

Photo credits

Front Cover: © Darcy Kiefel/Kiefelphotography.com. **Back Cover:** © Zbigniew Bzdak/The Image Works. **Title Page:** p.1: © Digital Vision/Alamy. **Portrait Gallery:** p. 2: top, © Sue Cunningham/DanitaDelimont.com; center right, © Leanne Temme/Photolibrary; bottom left, © Wolfgang Kaehler. p. 3: top left, © Sean Sprague/The Image Works; top right, © Russell Gordon; bottom left, © Darcy Kiefel/Kiefelphotography.com. **Foreword:** p. 4: © Oryx Multimedia. **Love:** p. 6: left, © CedarBough Saeji; center, © David Rothschild. p. 7: top, © Russell Gordon; bottom, © Ellen Senisi/The Image Works. **Listen:** p. 8: © Ariadne van Zandbergen/AfriPics.com; p. 9: top left, © David Harry Stewart/Getty Images; bottom left, © Sonda Dawes/The Image Works; bottom right, © Wayne Eastep/Getty Images. **Explore:** p. 10: left, © DAJ/Imagestate; right, © B&C Alexander/Arcticphoto.com. p. 11: © Doranne Jacobson. **Stories:** p. 12: left, © Nativestock.com/Marilyn Angel Wynn; right, © Tami Kauakea Winston/Photo Resource Hawaii. p. 13: © Pascal Meunier. **Play:** p. 14: left, © Sean Sprague/The Image Works; center, © Carrie Niland/Syracuse Newspapers/The Image Works. p. 15: right, © Andy Ridder/ Photolibrary. **Teach:** p. 16: © Lawrence Migdale/Photo Researchers, Inc. p. 17: left, © Walter Hodges/Photolibrary; top right, © John Warburton-Lee/DanitaDelimont.com; bottom right, © Eastcott-Momatiuk/The Image Works. **Learn:** p. 18: left, © Jenny Matthews/Alamy; right, © David R. Frazier/DanitaDelimont.com. p. 18: © Darcy Kiefel/Kiefelphotography.com. **Celebrate:** p. 20: left, © 2010 Kayte Deioma; center, © Frans Lemmens/Lonely Planet Images. p. 21: right, © Jewish Chronicle Ltd/HIP/The Image Works. **Share:** p. 22: © Richard Lord/ The Image Works. p. 23: left, © B&C Alexander/Arcticphoto.com; right, © Mitch Wojnarowicz/Amsterdam Recorder/The Image Works. **Care:** p. 24: left, © Jeffrey Aaronson/Still Media; center, © Mike Greenlar/Syracuse Newspapers/The Image Works. p. 25: right, © Alison Wright. **Happy. Safe. Loved:** p. 26: left, © Art Wolfe/Artwolfe.com; right, © Darcy Kiefel/Kiefelphotography.com. p. 27: © Darcy Kiefel/Kiefelphotography.com. **Map:** p. 28: top left, © Elizabeth Crews/The Image Works; bottom right, © Ric Ergenbright/DanitaDelimont.com. p. 29: bottom left, © Nancy Grace Horton; top right, © Alison Wright. **Back Matter:** p. 30: © Alan Hicks/Getty Images. p. 31: left, © Bert Wiklund; right, © Celia Mannings/Alamy.

Text copyright © 2010 by The Global Fund for Children
Photographs copyright © 2010 by individual copyright holders
All rights reserved, including the right of reproduction in whole or in part in any form.
Charlesbridge and colophon are registered trademarks of Charlesbridge Publishing, Inc.

Developed by The Global Fund for Children
1101 Fourteenth Street NW, Suite 420
Washington, DC 20005
(202) 331-9003
www.globalfundforchildren.org

Published by Charlesbridge
85 Main Street
Watertown, MA 02472
(617) 926-0329
www.charlesbridge.com

Part of the proceeds from this book's sales will be donated to The Global Fund for Children to support innovative community-based organizations that serve the world's most vulnerable children and youth. Details about the donation of royalties can be obtained by writing to Charlesbridge Publishing and The Global Fund for Children.

Library of Congress Cataloging-in-Publication Data
Ajmera, Maya.
    Our grandparents : a global album / Maya Ajmera, Sheila Kinkade, Cynthia Pon.
        p. cm.
    ISBN 978-1-57091-458-4 (reinforced for library use)
    ISBN 978-1-57091-459-1 (softcover)
1. Grandparents—Juvenile literature. 2. Grandparent and child—Juvenile literature.
3. Grandchildren—Juvenile literature. I. Kinkade, Sheila, 1962– II. Pon, Cynthia. III. Title.
HQ759.9.A427 2010
306.874'5—dc22   2009005494

Printed in Korea
(hc) 10 9 8 7 6 5 4 3 2 1
(sc) 10 9 8 7 6 5

Display type and text type set in Century Schoolbook and Grilled Cheese
Color separations by Chroma Graphics, Singapore
Printed by Sung In Printing in Gunpo-Si, Kyonggi-Do, Korea
Production supervision by Brian G. Walker
Designed by Susan Mallory Sherman